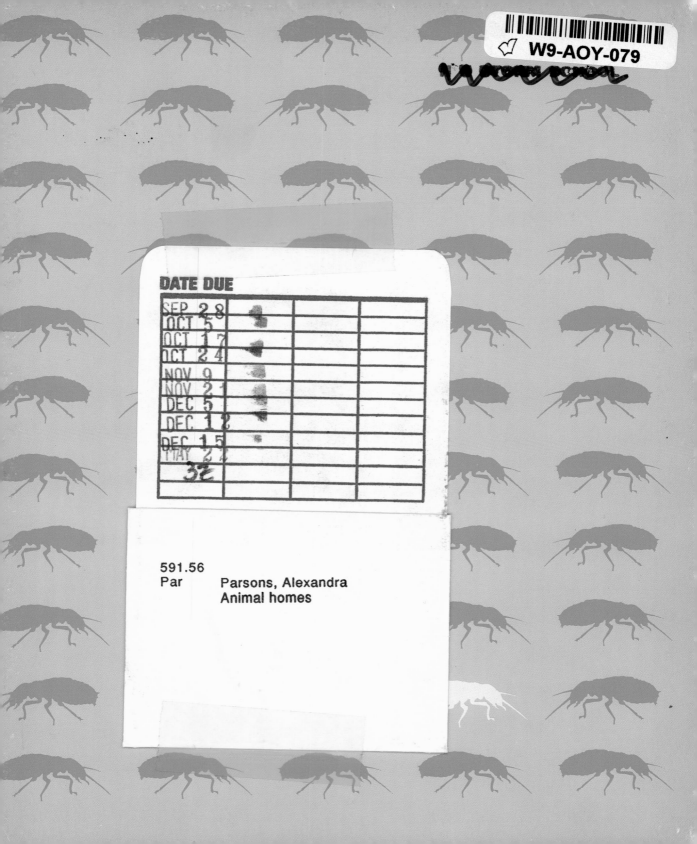

A DORLING KINDERSLEY BOOK

Conceived, edited, and designed by DK Direct Limited

Note to parents

What's Inside? Animal Homes is designed to help young children understand what goes on inside some remarkable animal habitats. It shows how the oven bird's nest gives the bird its name, where bees store their food, and how termites build their rock-hard mounds. It is a book for you and your child to read and talk about together, and to enjoy.

Editor Hilary Hockman
Designer John Strange
Typographic Designer Nigel Coath
U.S. Editor Laaren Brown

Illustrators Stuart Lafford/Linden Artists,
Michelle Ross/Linden Artists
Photographer Kevin Mallett
Written by Alexandra Parsons
Consultant Theresa Greenaway
Design Director Ed Day
Editorial Director Jonathan Reed

Picture Credits Heather Angel (pp. 9, 16), Jane Burton/Bruce Coleman Ltd. (cover, pp. 2, 13),
Luiz Claudio Marigo/Bruce Coleman Ltd. (p. 4), Pictures For Print (p.14), Andy Price/Bruce Coleman Ltd. (p. 6),
Hans Reinhard/Bruce Coleman Ltd. (p. 8), F. Saver/Bruce Coleman Ltd. (p. 17), Gunter Ziesler/Bruce Coleman Ltd. (p. 5)

First American Edition, 1993

10 9 8 7 6 5 4 3 2 1

Published in the United States by
Dorling Kindersley, Inc., 232 Madison Avenue
New York, New York 10016

Library of Congress Cataloging-in-Publication Data
Animal Homes. – 1st American ed.
p. cm. – (What's inside?)
Summary: Text and pictures take the reader inside different animal homes,
including a beaver's lodge, an oven bird's nest and a trapdoor spider's burrow.
ISBN 1-56458-218-3
1. Animals – Habitations – Juvenile literature. [1. Animals – Habitations.] I. Series.
QL756.A534 1993
591.56'4 — dc20   92–54271 CIP AC

Printed in Italy

WHAT'S INSIDE?
ANIMAL HOMES

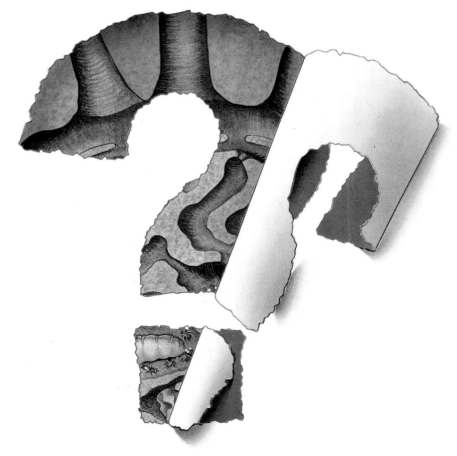

DORLING KINDERSLEY
LONDON • NEW YORK • STUTTGART

BEEHIVE

A beehive is abuzz with activity! Thousands of bees live here. Their hive is made of hundreds of tiny wax cells that fit neatly together to save space. The hive is organized so the bees can rear their young and store their food in it.

There are three kinds of bees in a beehive. One queen bee lays all the eggs – up to 1,500 a day. The hundred or so drone bees are male. They have no stinger and just buzz around all day, doing very little. The rest are worker bees.

Wild honeybees build new hives in the summer. They choose shady spots, like this one in a hollow tree.

Wax for building the hive comes from special glands inside the worker's abdomen. It comes out as flakes of fatty stuff, which the worker softens by chewing.

A nest is built by thousands of worker bees that spend their short lives just working. They are females, but they never lay eggs.

Worker bees build
hanging panels of
six-sided wax cells.

Worker bees collect
pollen from flowers.
It's stored in these cells.

Bees make honey from the
sweet nectar of flowers.
The honey is stored in cells,
each protected by a wax lid.
Honey is the bees' winter food.

The queen bee buzzes
around, laying eggs
in the empty cells.

Worker bees in charge of
the nursery feed the young
grubs in the nursery cells.
The grubs eat pollen, nectar,
or royal jelly. A gland in the
worker's head produces the
royal jelly.

If a female is fed on royal jelly, she will develop into
a queen. If she is just fed on nectar and pollen, she will
develop into a worker. The males all end up as drones.

OVEN BIRD'S NEST

These birds live in Central and South America. Their round, oven-shaped nests are made from mud, fur, hair, grass, and straw. They build them during damp weather when there is plenty of soft mud for them to use. After the damp weather, the sun comes out and bakes the mud hard, like a clay pot.

Like most birds, the oven bird uses its beak and feet to build its nest. The bird collects a pellet of mud in its beak and mixes it with straw ...

... then flattens the pellet and pushes it into place with its feet and beak.

There are six different kinds of oven bird. This one is from South America, where it is known as *el hornero* – Spanish for baker.

This *hornero* has built its nest high up on the top of a post, but other oven birds build in trees, in old cooking pots ... even on the ground if there are no trees.

Twice a year, in the breeding seasons, this oven bird lays two to six eggs. They hatch after two weeks, and two weeks later the baby birds will be ready to fly away.

The nests are very strong and can last several years.

Egg-eating animals like snakes have trouble getting into the nest, thanks to a wall just inside the entrance.

The eggs are laid on a soft bed of grass, feathers, or moss. They are out of harm's reach in the inner chamber.

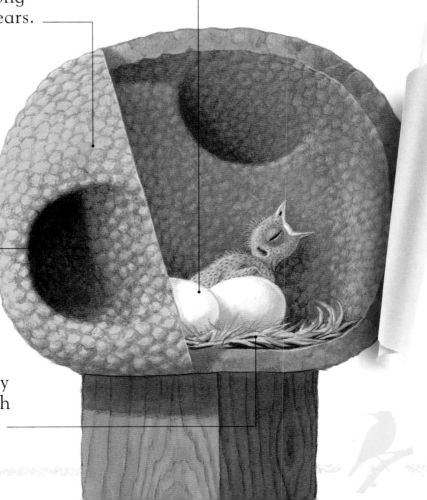

5

TERMITE MOUND

Termites are related to cockroaches, but they behave more like ants. They live and work together in huge termite mounds. The biggest are in Australia and Africa. These amazing nests are like air-conditioned cities protected by rock-hard walls.

Termites come in all shapes and sizes because they all have different jobs to do. The king and queen busy themselves with the egg-laying ...

... the soldiers and workers do everything else. As you might have guessed, the mound is built by the workers!

The worker termite has powerful jaws. It uses its jaws and front legs to scoop up mud. Then it mixes the mud with saliva to make its home-building material.

A termite mound may last more than 50 years. Generation after generation of termites can live in the same mound.

Here's some food – fungus from an underground fungus garden. Yummy!

Termites like it hot, but not too hot! Warm air comes up from the nest and goes through these chimneys to the outside.

Baby termites hatch in special nurseries.

The walls of the nest are made from the workers' saliva and mud.

Termites go in and out of their fortress home along these tunnels.

Here's the queen – a bloated, egg-laying sausage up to 7 inches long ...

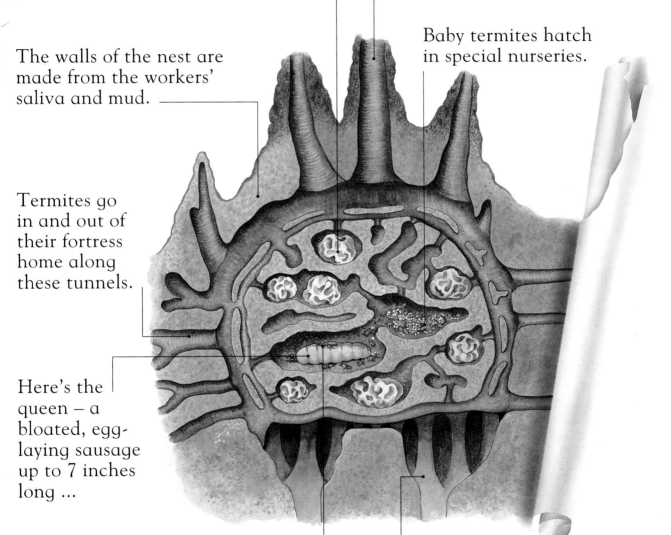

... and this is her king. The king and queen live in the royal chamber at the heart of the termite city.

These shafts go down into damp earth below the mound so that workers can collect water.

BEAVER LODGE

Beavers are the engineers of the animal kingdom. They chop down trees to make dams across streams and small rivers. The dams turn fast-flowing streams into calm, shallow lakes – the perfect spot for a beaver lodge.

Look at these sharp front teeth. A beaver can bite and chop its way through a small tree in minutes.

The strong claws on its front paws are for digging and carrying.

Back feet are webbed – just right for swimming.

The beaver wedges strong timbers into the riverbank and riverbed. It builds its dam of sticks, stones, and mud on top of this.

With its lodge in the middle of a pool, the beaver family is protected from its enemies. The underwater entrance is well hidden.

The mud floor of the lodge is kept clean and dry. Young beaver kits stay safely inside until they are nearly two months old.

Fresh air comes in through an air shaft.

The lodge is made of sticks and stones, cemented together with mud and grass.

The beaver reaches the lodge via underwater tunnels.

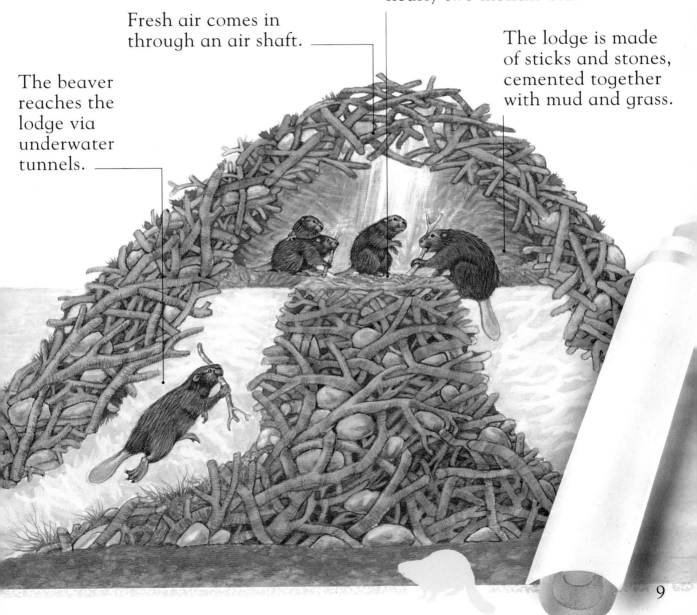

SPIDER'S BURROW

Most spiders spin webs, then hang around just out of sight,
waiting for lunch to fly in. Not the trapdoor spider!
This remarkable spider digs a burrow, lines it with silk,
and seals it with a trapdoor. Then out it pounces, like a
jack-in-the-box, to grab any unsuspecting passing bug.

Trapdoor spiders
use their jaws to
dig burrows.

The trapdoor stops earth, dust,
rain, and unwelcome visitors
from getting inside the burrow.

Claws on the ends of the
spider's feet help it climb up
the silk lining of the burrow –
just like climbing a ladder.

The spider makes liquid silk in special
glands inside its body. The liquid
hardens into a strong thread when it
comes out of these spinnerets.

The door is made of layers of silk and soil. It's topped with a disguising layer of moss or leaves.

The door has a hinge of silk.

The spider hooks its claws into the silk on the underside of the door to hold it shut. That's in case its worst enemy, the large sand wasp, should come strolling by.

First the spider lines its burrow with soil and saliva. Then it makes a beautiful inner lining of silk.

The female lays her eggs in a silken purse attached to the burrow lining.

The baby spiders will stay with their mother until they are about eight months old. Then they are ready to leave and dig their own burrows.

RABBIT WARREN

A rabbit warren can be home to dozens of rabbits and their babies. It's made of lots of underground burrows and tunnels. You can see rabbits mostly in the early morning or evening, hopping about the fields nibbling grass. The minute one of them senses danger, it thumps its back feet on the ground – and all the rabbits disappear as if by magic.

Female rabbits are the ones who do most of the digging to make the burrows.

This tunnel with a dead end is called a bolt-hole. It's a hiding place.

They scrabble away at the earth with their front paws ...

... and push all the earth up to the surface with their strong back legs.

Rabbit warrens are usually dug into sandy banks, or in and around tree roots in open woodland.

Sometimes a mother has to leave her kits alone while she goes out to find food. She covers the entrance to the burrow with earth and grass to keep her little ones well hidden.

Mother rabbit looks after her young babies, or kits, in a separate breeding burrow. She makes the burrow cozy with dry grass and soft fur picked from her coat.

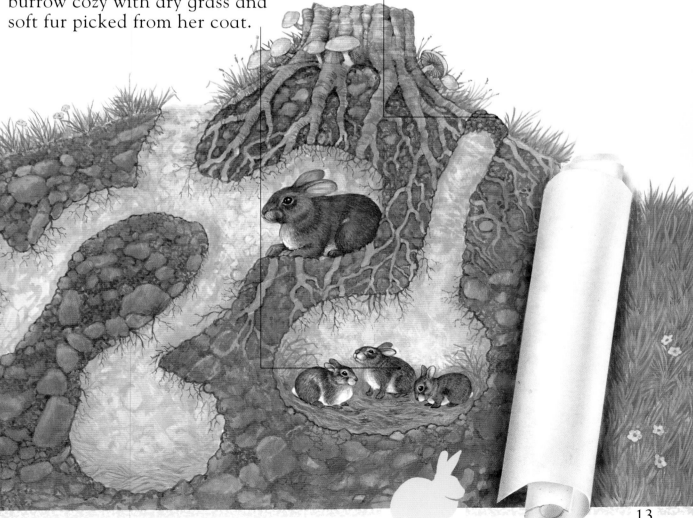

SQUIRREL'S NEST

Most squirrels live in the woods, where there are plenty of soft leaves and twigs for building nests, and lots of nuts and seeds for food. It can take as long as five days to build a good, safe nest. In winter, squirrels crawl in to keep warm and to snooze. In summer, the squirrels' nests are full of babies.

The squirrel's nest-building tools are its front teeth, nose, and mouth.

Squirrels live either in dens, which are built in tree hollows, or in dreys, which are a bit like birds' nests. Dreys are built high in the trees, wedged securely between branches.

The outer part of the drey is made of woven twigs and leaves. Squirrels cut the twigs with their sharp little teeth.

Baby squirrels are born hairless, blind, and deaf, so they need tender loving care. They will be ready to move out of the nest when they are between 10 and 14 weeks old.

Mother squirrels usually have three babies in a litter.

To make the drey warm and comfy, the squirrels line it with dry, springy mosses, dried grasses, sheep's wool, soft feathers, and warm thistledown.

The drey is built on a platform of woven twigs. Squirrels will choose a place that is sheltered from the wind.

A BORROWED HOME

The smallest crab in the world – the pea crab – has solved its housing problem by becoming a boarder! For protection, the pea crab lives sometimes in the shell of a live oyster, sometimes in a scallop or in a sea urchin, but most often in a mussel.

The tough, blue-black shell protects the mussel – and its pea crab – from the pounding of the sea on rocks.

Mussels use strong, gluey thread to stick themselves to rocks.

The male pea crab measures barely a quarter of an inch across. He swims in and out of different mussels any time he feels like it.

The female is bigger and stays in one mussel home. She lays her eggs inside, and passing water currents carry the eggs away.

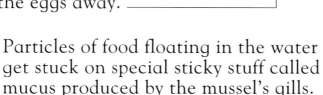

Particles of food floating in the water get stuck on special sticky stuff called mucus produced by the mussel's gills.

Tiny hairs on the gills, called cilia, push the water (with its food particles) toward the mussel's mouth.

And guess where the pea crab sits? Right here, among the mussel's gills, so it can snatch tempting morsels as they pass.

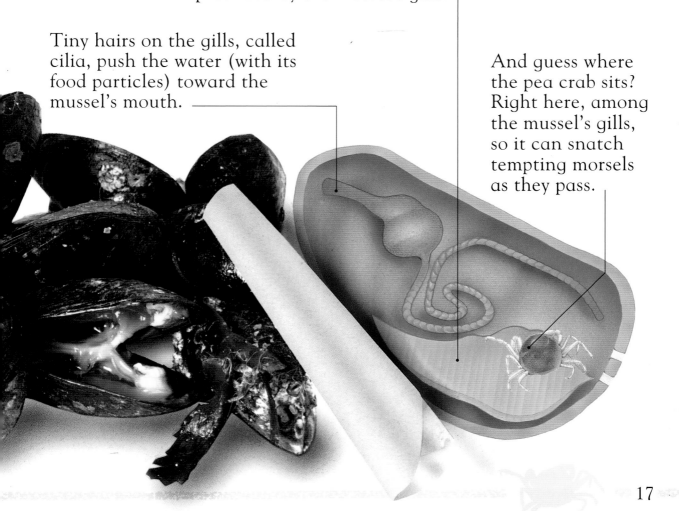